W9-BME-444

Hot Pot

The Sound of Short O

By Cynthia Amoroso

It is fun to help
Mom cook.

A pot helps make food hot.

We can fill the pot with corn on the cob.

Where is a top to cover the pot?

I can see the
pot get hot.

11

Can you hear the bubbles pop?

What other things cook in the pot?

This pot can hold a lot!

When it is full, it is time to stop.

19

Time to wash the pot!

Word List:

cob   pop

hot   pot

lot   stop

Mom   top

Note to Parents and Educators

The books in this series are based on current research, which supports the idea that our brains are pattern-detectors rather than rules-appliers. This means children learn to read easier when they are taught the familiar spelling patterns found in English. As children encounter more complex words, they have greater success in figuring out these words by using the spelling patterns.

Throughout the series, the texts provide the reader with the opportunity to practice and apply knowledge of the sounds in natural language. The books introduce sounds using familiar onsets and *rimes*, or spelling patterns, for reinforcement.

For example, the word *cat* might be used to present the short "a" sound, with the letter *c* being the onset and "_at" being the rime. This approach provides practice and reinforcement of the short "a" sound, as there are many familiar words made with the "_at" rime.

The stories and accompanying photographs in this series are based on time-honored concepts in children's literature: well-written, engaging texts and colorful, high-quality photographs combine to produce books that children want to read again and again.

Dr. Peg Ballard
Minnesota State University, Mankato

The Child's World®
childsworld.com

Published by The Child's World®
1980 Lookout Drive • Mankato, MN 56003-1705
800-599-READ • www.childsworld.com

ACKNOWLEDGMENTS
The Child's World®: Mary Berendes, Publishing Director
The Design Lab: Design
Michael Miller: Editing

PHOTO CREDITS
© Africa Studio/Shutterstock.com: cover; BrandX: 6;
Coprid/iStockphoto.com: 9; dem10/iStockphoto.com: 5;
domin_domin/iStockphoto.com: 21; fstop123/iStockphoto.
com: 2; letty17/iStockphoto.com: 14; sumnersgraphicsinc/
iStockphoto.com: 18; ttatty/iStockphoto.com: 17;
wandee007/Shutterstock.com: 10, 13

ISBN 9781634070232
LCCN 2015930167

Printed in the United States of America
Mankato, MN
July, 2015
PA02267

ABOUT THE AUTHOR

Cynthia Amoroso holds undergraduate degrees in English and elementary education, and graduate degrees in curriculum and instruction as well as educational administration. She is currently an assistant superintendent in a suburban metropolitan school district. Cynthia's past roles include teacher, assistant principal, district reading coordinator, director of curriculum and instruction, and curriculum consultant. She has extensive experience in reading, literacy, curriculum development, professional development, and continuous improvement processes.